ParentPreneur Survival Guide

(Quick Guide)

By Juliet N. Jones, MBA/CHRM/CEL

Copyright @ 2019 by Juliet N. Jones

All rights reserved. No part of this book may be reproduced in any form or by any electronic or mechanical means including information storage and retrieval systems without written permission from the Author, except in case of a reviewer, who may quote brief passages embodied in critical articles or in a review.

Trademark names appear throughout and used in editorial fashion with no intention of infringement of the respective owners' trademark.

The information in this book is distributed on an "as is" basis, without warranty. Precautions were taken in preparation of this work, neither author nor publisher shall have any liability to any person or entity with respect to any loss or damage caused or alleged to be caused directly or indirectly by the information contained int his book.

All scripture quotations unless otherwise indicated is taken from the New King James Version, 1982 by Thomas Nelson, Inc. with all rights reserved as well as any quotes and authors listed of that quote.

Printed in the US

Published by VIP Fortune 500 Consulting dba

VIP Fortune 500 Publishing

Parentpreneur Survival Guide

By: Juliet N. Jones   ISBN: 9781695468924

Table of Contents

- Dedication: **By Juliet N. Jones**
- Acknowledgement: **By Juliet N. Jones**
- Chapter 1: "***Surviving*** as a **ParentPreneur**"
- Chapter 2: Super Dad
- Chapter 3: Super Mom
- Chapter 4: Super Parents
- Chapter 5: What does your checklist look like?
- Chapter 6: It truly takes Faith!
- *Author/Biography*: ***About Juliet N. Jones***
- *Bibliography:* *Work Cited*

Dedication

This book is dedicated first and foremost to God (the Father, Son, and Holy Spirit). If it wasn't for God, I would not be able to live my best life now.

I give God all the Glory, Honor and Praise for allowing me to be a contributing factor in His plan, and His will while pursuing my dream(s) and spreading the good news. I'm thankful for my gifts and talents that come from God, and God alone. I am thankful for life, and his everlasting love. I also dedicate this book to my children Arielle and Juleon who are my biggest inspirations as they kept me going, even at times when they didn't realize it. I love you both beyond words unconditionally, and I encourage you daily to put God first, and to Dream-Build-Win! My journey as a Parentpreneur would not have been possible without the two of you.

Acknowledgements

By Juliet N. Jones

I acknowledge and thank my family. My mother Yvonne, father James, sister Kisha, my children Arielle and Juleon, nephews Maliek and Justin, and the rest of my siblings and family. I have a lot of family members on each side, and there are truly too many names to name each relative, but they know who they are as well as great friends whom I love and appreciated very much.

Congratulations to all of the Super Moms and Super Dads (single or married) in the world who are doing your best while juggling work, life, and parenting! In Today's society we see the "SHEroes and the HEroes', but we don't always see what happens "behind the scenes" of this juggling act (of work, life, and parenthood). This survival guide (quick guide) book is the all-in-one resource you need to create your "survival guide toolbox" with easy-to-use strategies, backed by real life stories, inspirational encouragement, and the tools needed for overcoming challenges faced by todays Parents who are Entrepreneurs aka - "Parentpreneurs'".

Be sure to grab a copy of the **"Parentpreneur Survival Guide Co-Author's Edition"** for extended stories, inspirations, and extended survival guide tools you won't want to miss out on!

Chapter 1
"*Surviving* as a *ParentPreneur*"
By Juliet N. Jones MBA/CHRM/CEL

Let me start off by saying that being an entrepreneur is hard work! Let me also add that being a parent is equally just as hard! Other parents, even single parents often make it look so easy. Who would of thought caring for, and/or raising another human being would be so much work?! However; on the flip side - it is one of the greatest gifts and blessings in the world, and I would not trade it for anything. Here are a few of my facts based on my own experience as a single mother of two amazing children at the time I wrote this Chapter, now age 18 (my son) and age 22 (my daughter). Let me share my truth:

- No, it was not easy!
- No, you are not going to go crazy despite what you feel some days!
- Yes, there were times I wanted to give up. That is normal, but don't!
- Absolutely there were times I cried because raising a child is super challenging! No one said it was truly going to be easy.
- No, you cannot do it without God! That is a fact. God keeps you from losing your mind (smiles).
- Yes, it is Possible to raise a child alone and/or with limited funds. I learned how to make a dollar out of 15 cents as they say.

I believe it takes a supernatural power that parents find deep within themselves that makes them a Super Mom or Super Dad. Further, it takes all the power from God to get through life especially juggling work and family (among other things) which is what led me to come up with the title of this book "ParentPreneur Survival Guide". We are out here trying to just survive daily. Most working parents could use a guide to help them survive and balance it all (work, life, ministry, family, you name it). I'm prayerful this book will be that guide for many parents to inspire, uplift, and encourage parents during their life journey as a parentpreneur! As a CEO, Author, Speaker, and Consultant I balance it all with my blueprints. My blueprints come from what I call the "**B**asic **I**nstructions **B**efore **L**eaving **E**arth" aka the B.I.B.L.E. God is the perfect parent, and he tells us exactly how to live and raise our children. That is our true "survival guide". My book is a compilation of experiences from others who not only applied God's word, but also shared their stories and tips of how they survived it all in efforts to help you in your process as you read this book. Keeping God over everything is the best way to start. Here are a few of God's guided word for us:

- Proverbs 22:6 - "Train up a child in the way he should go, and when he is old, he will not depart from it".

- Ephesians 6:4 - "Fathers, do not provoke your children to anger, but bring them up in the discipline and instruction of the Lord".

- "To discipline a child produces wisdom, but a mother is disgraced by an undisciplined child." Proverbs 29:15.

- "Sons/daughters are a heritage from the Lord, children a reward from him. Like arrows in the hands of a warrior are sons/daughters born in one's youth. Blessed is the man whose quiver is full of them." Psalm 127:3-5.

- "Jesus said, Let the little children come to me, and do not hinder them, for the kingdom of heaven belongs to such as these.'" Matthew 19:14.

Although I'm a working mother, it doesn't mean God and my family do not come first. See, "Work–Life Balance" is a phrase commonly used to describe the balance that a working parent needs between time allocated for work and time needed for other aspects of life (Wikipedia). It means there are times I struggle with having to decide which comes first, and that is never easy. Overall, family should come 1st at least 9 out of the 10 times. Always remember, maintaining a healthy balance is tough but also achievable!

Here's how to achieve a healthy work life balance in 5 steps:

Step 1: Prioritize work and life's tasks and make enough time to complete them.

Step 2: Structure time at work and at home with family.

Step 3: Take breaks during the workday, or personal day for needed R&R time for you to "recharge-refuel-restart". You can't be anything to anyone if you are not healthy enough to serve at work or home. It is essential to take care of you in the process!

Step 4: Make use of down time or holidays to recharge-refuel-restart and meditate on God's word and direction.

Step 5: Leverage technology to work smarter not harder.

Chapter 2
"Super Dad"

Super Dad:

I may not be a Dad, but I surely know plenty, (all types), and I see them in action in, and outside of my family and/or the workplace. I remember working in a corporate office, watching one  manager run out the door every day at exactly 4:59 pm on the dot. He didn't pass go nor collect $200 on the way. He had just had a brand new baby (him and his wife's first child), and he was determined not to miss a beat. The company we worked for often mandated hours for employees who were also in the same boat and missing out on their child's "precious moments, or events". Not by choice, but because they had to stay late at work for a big project or a deadline which took priority over their personal life. I could see the hurt in his eyes on the days he had to stay late against his better wishes as he slowly passed by my HR office, with half a frown, holding his clip board and wearing his managers hat ready to hit the shipping department - knowing there was only one place he would rather be, and that was at home! Now, I'm not talking about the workaholics who do the complete opposite, I'm talking about the dads who wanted to balance work and life.

My point to this is knowing "you are not alone" and sometimes you must accept things you cannot always control. Knowing you want to be home is a beautiful start. Knowing you want to be at your child's game, or out shopping together, or at their recitals, or tossing the ball in the backyard, or cooking a meal together, etc. Is what makes a good dad a "super dad" in my eyes. Anyone can be a father or father a child, but it takes someone special to be called "dad" especially a super dad.

Many fathers face a ton of challenges. It is how they respond to those challenges that make them super special! Remember you are only human, but your superhuman power in being able to own and carry out your role as a "Dad" while also overcoming life's obstacles with work while parenting. It is also being able to be the head of the household, your child's first encounter with a male as the role model for the son, and/or future husband role model for your daughter etc. It doesn't matter if you didn't have a father  to show you how to be a good dad. You still have a choice to do better and be better. We have 365 days in a year. That gives us all 365 opportunities to be great. Again, I'm no father, but from the fathers I do know including my own – you can start with loving unconditionally as God does. My advice to all dads is simple: do all that you can, when you can, and do the best with what you've got! God can and will handle the rest. When in doubt - repeat this Serenity Prayer! *Heavenly Father, Grant to us the serenity of mind to accept that which cannot be changed; courage to change that which can be changed, and wisdom to know the one from the other, through Jesus Christ our Lord, Amen.*

Chapter 3
"Super Mom"

Super Mom:

As a single mother and for "any mother" I've talked to, I've learned that you need to have the faith and patience of JOB from the Bible to not only birth a child, but to raise a child (and in some cases raise more than one alone or married). Needless to say, neither is a walk in the park. On top of that – there is working full time, and like myself "going after your dreams" while parenting. (so, hats off to moms who were "stay at home moms") as that is hard work as well, yet that was not me. I was working a full-time job, and parenting two children.

There are days you must pull from places you didn't even think you could pull from, in order to get to the next second, or the next minute - let alone the next day. My life was much like the superheroes in the movies which inspired the theme and title for this book. Some days I had to put on a super cape and become a more powerful resilient person in order to "juggle it all" as an entrepreneur and full-time mom. Sometimes, I would have those moments that just when you think you have saved the day - some villain (i.e.; I define villains such as: a past due bill, unfinished project, unforeseen circumstance, school event, missed bus, lost homework, dog needs let out, someone spilled juice on the cream colored carpet, siblings fighting, remote to the tv is misplaced, dishes in the sink, 7th school key cannot be found again, child's fever is still rising, son fell off his bike, daughter's periodic meltdowns, dreaded parent teacher conferences, delayed child support check, someone always needing money for something villain...I think you get the villains here)! Well, these villains would force you to nearly lose your mind OR go right into the superhero form you didn't even know you could morph into (like Wonder Women spinning around several times to get into uniform or Clark Kent turning into Superman). When the villains show up "speak Gods word" as the first weapon! Remember this scripture, as it helped me on many occasions. *Galatians 6:9: "And let us not grow weary while doing good, for in due season we shall reap, if we do not lose heart."* My point is don't grow weary. You can do it! Trust me.

Life just happens. Causing you to have to muster up the strength, put on your super mom cape, gear up, and defeat those challenges and /or villains. Here are two additional tools I use daily to help defeat those villains when they showed up many times, and Oh, yes - they will show up more than once. My favorite scriptures are:

- Matthew 19:26 - "With God, all things are possible".
- Philippians 4:13 – "I can do all things through Christ who strengthens me".

The objective is to know that no one is perfect and to not give up no matter what. I mentioned that earlier under the Super Dad section. Like Dorothy in the Wizard of Oz, I have had to click my heels, spin around, count to 10, 20 some days 100, pick my battles, and most of all "pray"! Yes, I called on Jesus many times especially when my children hit "teen years". As a single mom if I didn't call on Jesus, someone was going to get seriously hurt. I'm not sure about you, but there were days my children were like little angles. Then, there were days I wondered who are these kids? Especially when I would encounter the following scenarios:

- Doors slamming.
- Back talking.

- Elevated tones when speaking to me like they lost their minds.
- Bedroom not clean, dishes, house etc.
- Someone broke something and didn't know who did it (they always said "not me") which was ironic because there were only 2 of them in the house besides the dog.
- They had me in parent teacher meetings over unsatisfactory grades they failed to disclose to me before the school contacted me.
- Lying thinking I would never find out about the secret incidents.
- You name it – it happened.

There were times I not only cried, but I seriously was looking around saying Jesus you don't see this? Help me not go to jail Lord Jesus (smiles). I often wondered if Ashton K. was going to jump out on any given day and say I was being "punked" because some days it was "unreal". Guess what? I had a plan and a secret weapon (God) that they didn't know about, and never saw coming!

I didn't' always have my kids dad around to say "Call your father to deal with this", or "Your dad will get with you when he gets home" so I had to learn and /or do the following which helped me. It was not always my norm, but these new tactics truly did help such as:

- Parental Tip: yelling and/or screaming at children will only make the situation worse. Louder isn't better. Now, don't get me wrong I was raised old school by a mother who put me in my place first, and asked questions later in any volume. However; times have changed and are different. I learned that effective communication is just as impactful. So is taking away privileges until re-earned.

- Keep them active and busy. Sports, Jobs, Music lessons, and/or Mentorship programs! Children need to experience things outside of the home to also grow. As an Entrepreneur (singer, author, speaker, and business consultant), I would involve my children in my work. They assisted me when I was booked to sing or speak as my brand ambassadors! Keeping them involved in Church as well. I kept my children grounded in the word of God.
- Set boundaries and rules, and take the time to explain it to them just why the boundaries and rules are important.
- Give love, and it shall be given back to you.
- Remember you are their first teacher, so teach with love and patience. 1 *Corinthians 13: 4-7 tells us Love is patient, love is kind. It does not envy, it does not boast, it is not proud. It does not dishonor others, it is not self-seeking, it is not easily angered, it keeps no record of wrongs.*

I loved teaching my children about God, values, morals and life. All you can do as a parent is teach them right from wrong, and then pray that when they grow up, they will remember and use what they were taught and leave the rest in God's hands. Trust that it will be ok. I developed an attitude of gratitude, realizing it could be better yes, but it could also be worse. It's amazing what can happen when you allow God to "help you".
Juggling is not easy. Especially when you are not truly prepared to juggle multiple children or tasks. This day and age the man doesn't just bring home the bacon while the wife cooks it up in a pan. As for me, I'm a go getter so as a single mom I bring home the bacon and cook it. Is it easy? No way, not even a little, but it is possible. I encourage you to not give up. Think of the good things you have and the good things your children have

accomplished. Focus more on the positives versus the negatives. Use the experience as a training to get stronger and develop not just their weaknesses, but your own as well. I learned more about "me" in the process of parenting, then I did before I was a mom. I learned the following:

- Patience
- Strength
- Gratitude
- Time management and how to prioritize.
- It's ok to not always "feel ok". Afterall, we are only human.
- How to enjoy precious moments and create new ones.
- How to be thankful, honest, forgiving, and consistent.
- How to get closer to God when faced with challenges.
- And How to fight the enemy when he targeted me and my family. (Here's a tip it's called "Battle Ready Prayer" on YouTube) one more of my many weapons that work.

I can't stress this enough so I will say it again: Prayer truly does change things! With prayer, faith, affirmations, and keeping a little red book called "my daily calendar" I had this thing under control. Works wonders. My advice to you is to:

- Keep God 1st and read scriptures on parenting.
- Grab a little calendar and chore chart for your fridge.
- Know that "you are not alone" as there are many parents out there facing the same challenges as you are. Get connected with a local group for parental support.
- Pray so you are ready for the challenges that life will bring in general through your child/children, and "do not give up". It will pay off in the end. I promise you.

No one is exempt from the challenge, so get ready and know that you can do this! "The golden rule of parenting is to always show your children the kind of person you want them to be. Remember that children are impressionable" (Elizabeth Roxas).

Chapter 4
"Super Parents"

You live, and you learn. I don't care what anyone says or quotes. There is no Perfect Parent out there. Everyone defines parenting on their time and terms and what works for their household and their family. The same concept goes for today's Entrepreneur. Your business runs on vision, mission, and core values. What you get out of it is based on what you put into it. Parenting is often trial and error. What works for some may not work for others. To each his /her own as long as there is no child abuse as that is simply not tolerated nor acceptable. I'm not here to judge, but I will recommend you do it according to Gods word to keep your sanity, and remain out of jail (smiles).

Like I stated earlier, I have been through the teen stages TWICE! It's like they think you don't know anything, and they know it all. They forget I was born first, and those hormones! Those hormones (OMG) were the *"hormone villains"*, and those years were tough. It was like a superpower that was feeding my children crazy energy, and attacking my strength (like kryptonite to superman). I had to find a way to shield those unfamiliar mood swings, backlash, dementia (oh yes, they forget stuff), and my favorite "It wasn't me" syndrome. I had to get my team ready because I was being "outnumbered" by the many cells inside my children called hormones.

      Parenting takes a team (in my day, and I can't believe I just said "in my day" as I must be getting old) it took a village. That village was my aunts, uncles, and neighbors etc. teaming up with my parents to keep me in check. Here's a tip: form your own. My children already know I have eyes "everywhere". The Avengers superheroes could not defeat Thanos the villain one on one, so they did it as a team (and recruited as many others willing to help them). As an entrepreneur I promote team building. It takes a team to reach goals in business. Parenting is no different. Sometimes you must gather up everyone you can (family, friends, pastor, mentors etc.), and prepare to win this thing. You may not win the first time around, but you can always huddle up, restrategize and make an amazing comeback. Accepting defeat should never be an option especially for a parent. We are in charge and like my mom use to say, " I brought you in this world and I can take you out" or "While under my roof, I'm in charge". Recite that as many times as needed. Worked for me and may just work for you!

Chapter 5
"What Does your Checklist Look Like?"

Take the time to step back and recognize the effort that went into raising your child or children. Did you have a To do list? Was it helpful? What did you learn from having one? Did you ever create one? Well, I want you to list your top 5 favorites **To Do List** items below. Remember, aim to tackle one thing at a time, and always celebrate when you get things done. Accomplishing small goals on your list are still worth celebrating! Afterall, you are worth it.

Top 5 favorite To Do List items that you can do to include your children and make "getting things done" - fun for everyone!

1. _____

2. _____

3. _____

4. _____

5. _____

Take the time to remove the clutter. If your life is cluttered and unorganized you won't stand a chance. What worked for me was getting organized and having an action plan. Set priorities for yourself and your children. I would create games to help my children not only achieve a goal, but get rewarded for doing it. It was a win win for us all. For example, I asked them to do things around the house (outside of mandatory chores) and they would receive a small gift for doing so. Much like one who works who earns a paycheck.

They were so competitive they would try to outdo each other to see who could get the most gifts. Guess who won in the end? Yup, me! All of my to do items were met and my children learned how to earn something from hard work while having fun doing it. Teach your children how to organize tasks and set priorities. They learn by watching you - so always be on your "A" game. Leaders lead by example. It is important to have your business in order as well as your home. Teach your children skills needed to prepare them for the future. In doing so, you will be raising great future parents, and/or great future business leaders! Ask yourself the following:

- How will I remove the clutter in my life?
- How much time will I set aside to pray, and seek God on my action plan?

What activities can I create that will incorporate the children and make reaching goals achievable and exciting? We are told to have organization at work so why not at home? If you are in ministry or in business or have employees who report to you, then you already know the importance of a To Do List! It's like a job description listing each of the "expectations" that need to be met. Well, the same principle should be applied at home also. Don't just create a list for yourself, but also create them for your family. I used to have a "chores chart" hanging on my fridge. It was clear, and to the point. Daily my children knew what was expected, and when.

> Daddy's To Do List
> - ~~Donate old baby clothes~~
> - ~~Set up toddler bed~~
> - ~~Find a reliable baby-sitter~~
> - ~~Cancel Amazon diapers and wipes subscription~~
> - ~~Steam clean the floors~~
> - ★ Freeze the kids' credit
> - ~~Send birthday thank you cards~~
> - ~~Change the air filter~~
> - ~~Increase AT&T data plan~~
> - ~~Set up back security camera~~

It also listed consequences if chores were not done such as: (no outings, or loss of cell phone for a period of time etc.), and I communicated this to my children up front. It saved me time and everyone from headaches of unfinished expectations. Structure and Boundaries are powerful tools for parents when communicated efficiently. Now, my children hated the list, but it was necessary. I know employees who don't like the tasks they have to complete at work however; they know they need to do it regardless. This prepares children for the workforce as it starts at home. This teaches them hard work, and accountability. Remember to also reward them for completing tasks (and it doesn't have to be anything huge it can be a hug or a kind word), but be sure they are recognized for their accomplishments. It will earn you loyalty and deserved respect. Let's also not forget to incorporate and reward your spouse for those who are married. Your spouse is an essential role in the family. Learn to work together!

God's words to uplift, encourage, and inspire you!

List 7 things that you speak with wisdom and faithful instruction at work or at home such as Scriptures or Affirmations. Even If you don't have any - just jot down some new quotes that you plan to use to help you get through each challenging day - one day at a time:

1. _____

2. _____

3. _____

4. _____

5. _____

6. _____

7. _____

Insert 7 things you plan to do to "take care of you" during down times . Remember rest and relaxation are needed, and your health is important. I would pray, read, get massages, and treat myself to ice cream with my down time. How do you plan to use your down time for much needed breaks from parenting and work?

1. _____

2. _____

3. _____

4. _____

5. _____

6. _____

7. _____

Chapter 6
"It Truly Takes Faith"

"God will never leave you nor forsake you"

Overall remember God has you. Put God in the mix of everything. We have the privilege to enter into Gods presence and receive his mercy. You can Win your children to a relationship

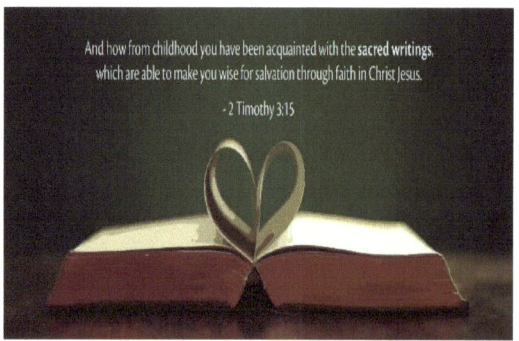

with God just by your actions. Our life of excellence and integrity is what speaks to their hearts. Keep your mind on God and move in faith. You are wonderfully made in Gods likeness and image. He called you to be an Entrepreneur (or an employee, minister, etc.), so whatever you do - know that it comes with much responsibility. If God also called you to be a parent, then that is another great assignment from God which means God trusts you with this assignment, and the ability to parent a child. All that is required of you is to place your trust in God knowing that God will never leave you nor forsake you. Scripture tells us that in God's presence there is fullness and joy, fullness of peace, fullness of victory and that is where you are refreshed and restored. God will certainly fill you with his love, joy, and strength so you can overcome any obstacles you face. God will forgive you of your past and/or past mistakes. Just ask his son Jesus to come into your heart, and help you to create a wonderful future and it will be so. There will always be mountains trying to get in the way, but God can and will go before you and level the mountains (Isaiah 45:2) . God is the real "Super Parent" so with God we are in good hands. God will help you through work, life, and parenting your child/children.

Lastly, here are a few additional quotes that I enjoyed reflecting on during my Parentpreneur journey:

"Being a family means you are a part of something very wonderful. It means you will love and be loved for the rest of your life." Lisa Weedn

"It didn't matter how big our house was; it mattered that there was love in it." Peter Buffett

"So even when it might seem easy to throw in the towel, just hang on. Things are a thousand times brighter on the other side and your children will be better for it." Unknown

"Parents can only give good advice or put them on the right paths, but the final forming of a person's character lies in their own hands." Anne Frank

"You don't have to be perfect, to be impactful" Juliet N. Jones

"You don't have to be great to get started, but you have to get started in order to be great" Zig Ziglar

Hey Dad and/or Moms: Congratulations on making it this far!
Love, Lead Author, Juliet N. Jones, CEO/MBA/CHRM/CEL

CEO @VIP Fortune 500 Consulting. Com

dba - Certified HR Experts .com / Also visit the Dream Build Win Academy Online Coaching at: www.ZeroToCEO . online

About the Lead Author

Juliet N. Jones Biography

By K. Ann Rawlings, PR Team for Juliet N. Jones

Juliet Nichole Jones, CEO/Author/Speaker/Consultant/Media

VIPFortune500ConsultingFirm.com/
VIPFortune500@yahoo.com

Juliet has 15+ years' Experience in
- Business Start Up
- Business Succession Planning, and expansion
- Human Resource Management / Outsourcing / Direct Hire
- Juliet has many years' experience in Media (On Air Radio Personality via iHeartMedia, and as Executive Board Member/Media Chairperson for the Greater Harrisburg Area NAACP)

Authored books include:
- Co-Author of Behind the Scenes of a Phenomenal Woman
- *Author* of Tired of being Tired (recharge-refuel-restart)

- *Author* of A Crash Course in Human Resources
- Co-Author of How to Make 5k in 30 days with the Glambitious team Partnership
- Co-Author of How to Win While you Wait with the Glambitious team Partnership
- *Author* of the ParentPreneur Survival Guide - Quick Guide
- *Lead Author* of the Parentpreneur – Co Author's Edition

Juliet Nichole Jones had become an inspiration for so many by sharing her story and captivating audiences on purpose driven tips and the 5 Secrets to Success!

Additionally, having shared the stage with other National Inspirational Speakers: Juliet has been nominated as Motivational Speaker of the year with SpeakerCon19 organization, received the 2017 Emerging Business of the Year award via Central Penn Business Journal, as well as shared the stage at the recent Suasion Leadercast event which featured Tyler Perry, and Andy Stanley. Juliet has also presented at Messiah College, Central Penn Business College, and has appeared on Cornerstone Television, Life Esteem via CBS 21, and various other national platforms. Juliet captivates her audience with her ability to explore some difficult topics, through transparency, honesty, warmth, and added humor. Juliet Jones is a thought provoking leader with a Master's in Business Administration, a CHRM, and Certification in Life Coaching and Executive Leadership - Juliet is an amazing storyteller with her ability to connect with and inspire her audience. She motivates other to take charge of their lives, and their business with her Dream-Build-Win model. She inspires others to realize their worth and potential they didn't know existed or never dreamed they could reach! Her Vision is to help dreamers, entrepreneurs and business owners succeed personally and/or professionally - with a Mission to empower others forward to Dream-Build-Win just like she did in going from Zero to CEO! Her favorite saying is "you don't have to be Great to get started, but you have to get started to be Great"! [Zig Ziglar].

Bibliography and/or Work Cited

Additional external Author's quoted:

- Elizabeth Roxas
- Lisa Weedn
- Peter Buffett
- Anne Frank
- Reinhold Niebuhr
- Zig Ziglar

Google images (various images/photos)

- Scriptures via Google and King James Version (bible)
- Bible verses, Pure Fli, Share Faith images, x and parental checklist, located: https://bitsofpositivity.com/best-quotes-encouragement-parents/

Insights/reference regarding Book Titled: Tired of being Tired, Recharge-Refuel- Restart by Juliet N. Jones 2019.

www.ingramcontent.com/pod-product-compliance
Lightning Source LLC
Chambersburg PA
CBHW040302220526
45473CB00002B/563